D0896734

SONGS OF DELIVERANCE

SONGS OF DELIVERANCE

Thirty-six New Hymns
by Timothy Dudley-Smith
Written since the publication of
LIFT EVERY HEART

Hodder & Stoughton
LONDON SYDNEY AUCKLAND TORONTO

Hope Publishing Company
CAROL STREAM, IL 60188

Hodder & Stoughton, Ltd.
Mill Road
Dunton Green
Sevenoaks, Kent
England TN13 2YA

Hope Publishing Company
Carol Stream, Illinois 60188, USA

First published 1988
ISBN
Hodder & Stoughton 0 340 43090 7
Hope Publishing Company 0 916642 35 6
Code No. 791
Library of Congress Catalog Card No. 88-80608

Printed in the U.S.A.

TIMOTHY DUDLEY-SMITH

*Thou art my hiding place; thou
shalt preserve me from trouble; thou
shalt compass me about with songs
of deliverance.*

Psalm 32.7

CONTENTS

Foreword

The titles given to collections of hymns form a study of their own. Today we seem to overwork the word 'Praise'. Earlier generations were more explicit. Anne Rennew (1714) called her hymns *Pious and Holy Breathings*. Richard Newman (1819), with becoming modesty, used as his title *Feeble attempts to praise God*. Earlier still had come *Seven Sobs of a Sorrowfull Soule for Sinne* (William Hunnis, d.1597) and *Goostly Psalmes and Spiritualle Songes* (Miles Coverdale, d.1568). I have chosen the title of this collection as a reminder that Christian hymnody has at its heart the Christian experience of forgiveness and of deliverance. As Erik Routley wrote on the final page of *Hymns Observed*, almost his last book:

> 'Those who write and compose hymns, those who edit the hymnals, and those who appoint them for worship and play and sing them are a team engaged in a business which no Christian age, and few religions of any kind, have regarded as irrelevent or unnecessary. Singing goes with whatever means most to people.'

This present book contains hymn texts written from the start of 1984, when my earlier collection *Lift Every Heart*[1.] went to press, until the end of 1987. During each of those four years I have been able to write eight or nine hymn texts, mostly during our summer holiday, and they form the body of this small book. I have followed the same principles of arrangement, indexing and so on as in my earlier collection; and have not repeated here what I said there about various issues in contemporary hymnody – my practice over 'inclusive' or archaic language for example. Similarly, the Index of biblical references includes, as before, only those passages which form the substantial basis of a hymn and does not set out to be a comprehensive list of biblical allusions or brief quotations.

Songs of Deliverance adds to, but does not attempt to update, what is to be found in *Lift Every Heart*. It is intended as a source book for editors and composers and those interested in contemporary hymnody; while making available to the more general reader texts which, with some exceptions, cannot at present be found elsewhere. My dream is that one day, in some years time, I may be able to produce a revised, updated and definitive Collection; but in the meantime I am very grateful to the Reverend Derek Kidner for much constructive encouragement and gentle criticism, and to Mr. George Shorney of the Hope Publishing Company and Mr. Tim Anderson of Hodder and Stoughton for making possible this publication.

Timothy Dudley-Smith
Ruan Minor, 1987

[1] Full details of *Lift Every Heart* will be found on the back cover. It is still in print on both sides of the Atlantic.

THE HYMNS

The hymn texts are not numbered, but are listed in alphabetical order both here and in the Notes (page 55). An index of first lines is included for easy reference at the back of the book (page 61).

A CITY RADIANT AS A BRIDE

based on Revelation 21, 22

A city radiant as a bride
   and bright with gold and gem,
a crystal river clear and wide,
   the new Jerusalem;
a city wrought of wealth untold,
   her jewelled walls aflame
with green and amethyst and gold
   and colours none can name.

A holy city, clear as glass,
   where saints in glory dwell.
Through gates of pearl her people pass
   to fields of asphodel.
In robes of splendour, pure and white,
   they walk the golden floor,
where God himself shall be their light
   and night shall be no more.

A city ever new and fair,
   the Lamb's eternal bride;
no suffering or grief is there
   and every tear is dried.
There Christ prepares for us a place,
   from sin and death restored,
and we shall stand before his face,
   the ransomed of the Lord.

ABOVE THE VOICES OF THE WORLD AROUND ME

Above the voices of the world around me,
my hopes and dreams, my cares and loves and fears,
the long-awaited call of Christ has found me,
the voice of Jesus echoes in my ears:
    'I gave my life to break the cords that bind you,
    I rose from death to set your spirit free;
    turn from your sins and put the past behind you,
    take up your cross and come and follow me.'

What can I offer him who calls me to him?
Only the wastes of sin and self and shame;
a mind confused, a heart that never knew him,
a tongue unskilled at naming Jesus' Name.
    Yet at your call, and hungry for your blessing,
    drawn by that cross which moves a heart of stone,
    now Lord I come, my tale of sin confessing,
    and in repentance turn to you alone.

Lord, I believe; help now my unbelieving;
I come in faith because your promise stands.
Your word of pardon and of peace receiving,
all that I am I place within your hands.
    Let me become what you shall choose to make me,
    freed from the guilt and burden of my sins.
    Jesus is mine, who never shall forsake me,
    and in his love my new-born life begins.

USA © 1987 by Hope Publishing Company, Carol Stream, IL 60188
World outside USA © 1985 by Timothy Dudley-Smith

ALMIGHTY LORD MOST HIGH DRAW NEAR

based on the Prayer of Manasseh

Almighty Lord Most High draw near
whose awesome splendour none can bear;
eternal God, in mercy hear,
receive once more the sinners' prayer;
    upon your word of grace we call
    whose word of power has ordered all.

How measureless your mercies stand,
the hope and pledge of sins forgiven;
those sins, unnumbered as the sand,
that hide the very stars of heaven:
    O God of grace, to us impart
    a penitent and contrite heart.

From such a heart we bend the knee
and all our sin and shame confess.
Lord, your unworthy servants see,
and clothe us round with righteousness;
    that loved and pardoned, healed and blest,
    we taste your mercies manifest.

So lift on high the Saviour's praise
with all the hosts of heaven above,
and sing through everlasting days
the God of glory, grace and love.
    The Lord of all let all adore,
    for ever and for evermore.

AN UPPER ROOM WITH EVENING LAMPS ASHINE

An upper room with evening lamps ashine,
the twelve disciples, and the table spread;
now in our turn Christ bids us pour the wine,
and in remembrance bless and break the bread.

We see by faith upon the cross displayed
his body broken and his blood outpoured;
in that dread robe of majesty arrayed
we gaze in worship on the dying Lord.

Dead for our sins, yet reigning now above:
still to our hearts we find his presence given;
take for ourselves the pledges of his love,
foretaste and token of that feast in heaven.

So send us out, to love and serve and praise,
filled with his Spirit, as the Master said:
love, joy and peace the wine of all our days,
Christ and his life our true and living bread.

USA © 1988 in SONGS OF DELIVERANCE by Hope Publishing Company, Carol Stream, IL 60188
World outside USA © 1987 by Timothy Dudley-Smith

APPROACH WITH AWE THIS HOLIEST PLACE

Approach with awe this holiest place,
the last of death's domain;
the shuttered heavens hide their face,
the powers of darkness reign;
    for there beneath those sombre skies
    the Prince of life, forsaken, dies.

The Prince of life! For us he came
from that high throne above,
his cross the measure of our shame,
his death the price of love;
    and at his cross, my soul, begin
    to feel the weight of love and sin.

Can this poor broken form be he
who taught the words of truth,
who strode the hills of Galilee
in all the flower of youth?
    Can this be he, this lifeless head,
    with grace and strength and beauty fled?

By wood and nails the work is done
that answers all our need,
the prize of full salvation won,
the ransomed sinner freed.
    Draw near with faith, my soul, and see
    the Prince of life who died for me.

The Prince of life! While time shall last
his cross and grave remain
sure signs of sin and sorrow past,
bright morning come again:
    an empty cross, an empty grave,
    a risen Christ to seek and save!

BE PRESENT, SPIRIT OF THE LORD

Be present, Spirit of the Lord,
  let sounds of earth be dumb:
the Father's love be shed abroad,
the dew of blessing on us poured –
  O silent Spirit, come!

In power unseen upon us rest,
  your gracious gifts impart:
a mind renewed, a spirit blessed,
a life where Christ is manifest,
  an understanding heart.

Love's sovereign work of grace fulfil,
  our souls to Christ incline,
intent to do the Father's will
and stand by faith before him still
  in righteousness divine.

O Spirit come, and with us stay;
  make every heart your home.
So work in us that we who pray
may walk with Christ in wisdom's way –
  O Holy Spirit, come!

USA © 1988 in SONGS OF DELIVERANCE by Hope Publishing Company, Carol Stream, IL 60188
World outside USA © 1984 by Timothy Dudley-Smith

BEHOLD A BROKEN WORLD, WE PRAY

based on echoes of Micah 4

Behold a broken world, we pray,
where want and war increase,
and grant us, Lord, in this our day,
the ancient dream of peace:

A dream of swords to sickles bent,
of spears to scythe and spade,
the weapons of our warfare spent,
a world of peace remade;

Where every battle-flag is furled
and every trumpet stilled,
where wars shall cease in all the world,
a waking dream fulfilled.

No force of arms shall there prevail
nor justice cease her sway;
nor shall their loftiest visions fail
the dreamers of the day.

O Prince of peace, who died to save,
a lost world to redeem,
and rose in triumph from the grave,
behold our waking dream.

Bring, Lord, your better world to birth,
your kingdom, love's domain;
where peace with God, and peace on earth,
and peace eternal reign.

BELOVED IN CHRIST BEFORE OUR LIFE BEGAN

based on Jeremiah 29.11

B eloved in Christ before our life began,
and from our wayward wanderings restored,
God has for each a purpose and a plan:
'I will fulfil my promise,' says the Lord.

Seek him and find him, then, with all your powers;
good and not evil has the Lord in store.
A future hope, a destiny is ours,
and, in his glory, life for evermore.

USA © 1988 in SONGS OF DELIVERANCE by Hope Publishing Company, Carol Stream, IL 60188
World outside USA © 1985 by Timothy Dudley-Smith

BLESS THE LORD, CREATION SINGS

from the Benedicite

Bless the Lord, creation sings;
earth and sky his hand proclaim.
Praise him, all created things;
angel hosts, exalt his Name.

Bless the Lord! To heaven's throne
songs of endless glory rise;
in the clouds his praise be shown,
sun and moon and starry skies.

Bless the Lord with ice and snow,
bitter cold and scorching blaze,
floods and all the winds that blow,
frosty nights and sunlit days.

Bless the Lord in mist and cloud,
lightnings shine to mark his way;
thunders speak his Name aloud,
wind and storm his word obey.

Bless the Lord who brings to birth
life renewed by sun and rain;
flowing rivers, fruitful earth,
bird and beast on hill and plain.

Bless the Lord! From earth and sky,
ocean depths and furthest shore,
all things living bear on high
songs of praise for evermore.

Bless the Lord! His Name be blessed,
worshipped, honoured, loved, adored;
and with holy hearts confessed,
saints and servants of the Lord.

Bless the Lord! The Father, Son,
and the Holy Spirit praise;
high exalt the Three in One,
God of everlasting days!

CHRIST IS RISEN AS HE SAID

an Easter antiphon

Choir:	Christ is risen as he said,
All:	Christ the firstborn from the dead:
C.	See, the stone is rolled away,
A.	see the place where Jesus lay.
C.	Lord of life, who lives again;
A.	Lord of lords, to rule and reign:
C.	Every tongue confess him now,
A.	every knee before him bow.
C.	Christ who died our life to win,
A.	Christ has conquered death and sin:
C.	Now is all his warfare done,
A.	now is every triumph won.
C.	Son of God, his life he gave,
A.	Son of man, to seek and save:
C.	Risen now, the Son who died,
A.	risen, ascended, glorified.

COME AND SEE WHERE JESUS LAY

'He is not here: for he is risen,
as he said. Come, see the place where
the Lord lay. And go quickly, and
tell his disciples that he is risen
from the dead . . .'
Matthew 28. 6,7

Come and see where Jesus lay,
    cold within the silent cave.
See, the stone is rolled away,
    void and tenantless the grave:
clothes to shroud his form and head
    still their absent Lord display;
Christ is risen from the dead!
    Come and see where Jesus lay.

Go and tell that Jesus reigns!
    Sin and death are overthrown.
Dead to sin and all its pains,
    live to make his glories known.
Raised in triumph, as he said,
    he who all the world sustains,
Christ is risen from the dead!
    Go and tell that Jesus reigns!

EYE HAS NOT SEEN, NOR EAR HAS HEARD

Eye has not seen, nor ear has heard,
  nor can the mind conceive
what God has pledged within his word
  for those he bids believe.

The secret things of God above
  to faith by wisdom shown,
the sacred mysteries of love,
  his Spirit now makes known.

Such love fulfilled its holiest part
  when Christ was crucified:
the flower of love's eternal heart,
  the Lord of glory died.

He died to do the Father's will,
  he rose by love's design,
he ever lives, immortal still,
  the Prince of life divine.

His immemorial purpose done,
  what blessings yet unfold!
Shall he who gave his only Son
  another gift withhold?

All things are ours! Our life restored
  is one with Christ above:
and ours, for ever with the Lord,
  the hidden depths of love.

FOR PEACE WITH GOD ABOVE

based on Philippians 4

For peace with God above
and every sin forgiven,
for all our hope of heaven,
we lift our hearts in love.

The peace of God be ours
enfolding every part,
possessing thought and heart,
the will and all its powers.

The God of peace defend
and keep us all our days
unwearied in his praise,
whose peace shall never end.

USA © 1988 in SONGS OF DELIVERANCE by Hope Publishing Company, Carol Stream, IL 60188
World outside USA © 1984 by Timothy Dudley-Smith

FROM ALL THE WIND'S WIDE QUARTERS

based on Isaiah 55

From all the wind's wide quarters
come, see the feast is spread,
of soul-sustaining waters,
of true and living bread;
of sorrows long-departed,
and joys beyond compare –
   come, poor and humble-hearted,
the feast of life to share!

With mercy all-prevailing
God bids the wanderer come;
in grace and peace unfailing
he calls his children home;
with loving-kindness tender
he frees us from our sins –
   in glory and in splendour
the feast of life begins!

Come, claim the promise spoken!
God's purpose stands secure.
His fruitful word unbroken
shall evermore endure.
All ancient bondage ended
to sin's corrupting powers –
   forgiven, freed, befriended,
the feast of life is ours!

USA © 1988 in SONGS OF DELIVERANCE by Hope Publishing Company, Carol Stream, IL 60188
World outside USA © 1984 by Timothy Dudley-Smith

FROM THE FATHER'S THRONE ON HIGH

based on Mark 13. 24-27

From the Father's throne on high
Christ returns to rule and reign.
Child of earth, he came to die;
Judge of all he comes again.

Darkened be the day at noon
when the stars of heaven fall:
earth and sky and sun and moon –
cloudy darkness covers all.

Ancient powers of sin and death
shake to hear the trumpet blown;
from the winds' remotest breath
God will gather in his own.

So behold the promised sign,
sky and sea by tumult riven,
and the King of kings divine
coming in the clouds of heaven.

Come then, Lord, in light and power,
at whose word the worlds began;
in the unexpected hour
come in glory, Son of man!

FROM THE NIGHT OF AGES WAKING

From the night of ages waking
  morning comes to heart and mind,
day of grace in splendour breaking,
mists and shadows fall behind;
  in the brightness of his glory
Christ the Light of life has shined.

Christ in light immortal dwelling,
Word by whom the worlds were made;
Light of lights, our dark dispelling,
Lord of lords in light arrayed;
  in the brightness of his glory
see the Father's love displayed.

Risen Lord in radiance splendid,
Christ has conquered Satan's sway;
sin and shame and sorrow ended,
powers of darkness flee away;
  in the brightness of his glory
walk as children of the day.

Light to lighten every nation,
shining forth from shore to shore,
Christ who won the world's salvation
now let all the earth adore;
  in the brightness of his glory
Light of life for evermore.

USA © 1988 in SONGS OF DELIVERANCE by Hope Publishing Company, Carol Stream, IL 60188
World outside USA © 1987 by Timothy Dudley-Smith

GIVE THANKS TO GOD ON HIGH

Give thanks to God on high
for saints of other days,
whose hope it was to live and die
in love's consuming blaze,
    for Christ and his kingdom,
his glory and his praise.

Their vision long-fulfilled,
our prayer is still the same;
upon their work of faith to build,
their word of truth proclaim,
    for Christ and his kingdom,
and for his holy Name.

New tasks today are ours
who serve a world in pain,
new calls to challenge all our powers
of heart and hand and brain,
    for Christ and his kingdom,
while life and breath remain.

Give thanks to God on high
for all the future sends,
in praise of Christ to live and die
who calls his servants friends,
    for Christ and his kingdom,
whose glory never ends!

USA © 1985 by Hope Publishing Company, Carol Stream, IL 60188
World outside USA © 1984 by Timothy Dudley-Smith

GOD AND FATHER, EVER GIVING

God and Father, ever giving
from the fruitful dust of earth
form and flesh to all things living,
life and being, breath and birth,
  living Lord, whose life we share,
  lift our hearts in love and prayer.

Son of God who came and sought us,
shared our pleasure and our pain,
who in dying loved and bought us
and triumphant rose again,
  living Lord, whose life we share,
  lift our hearts in love and prayer.

Holy Spirit, life bestowing,
breath of God on all our ways,
wind of heaven, freely blowing,
fire to set the soul ablaze,
  living Lord, whose life we share,
  lift our hearts in love and prayer.

God eternal, all sustaining,
King immortal, throned above,
Father, Son and Spirit reigning,
One in everlasting love,
  living Lord, whose life we share,
  lift our hearts in love and prayer.

USA © 1988 in SONGS OF DELIVERANCE by Hope Publishing Company, Carol Stream, IL 60188
World outside USA © 1987 by Timothy Dudley-Smith

GOOD NEWS OF GOD ABOVE

Good news of God above
is ours to tell abroad,
the Father's everlasting love
in Christ the risen Lord.
For neighbours near and far
the seed of life is sown;
then spread the seed
by word and deed
to make the Saviour known.

The love of Christ proclaim
who left his home on high;
to live our human life he came,
our human death to die.
The Father's only Son
became the sinners' friend,
our lot to share,
our sin to bear,
and death's dominion end.

The Lord of glory lives!
From cross and death and grave
his own abundant life he gives
to those he died to save.
His righteousness and peace
declare from sea to sea;
his praises sound
the world around
for Christ has made us free.

Hear now the Master's word
to those who bear his Name:
'So send I you,' till all have heard,
'make known, declare, proclaim.'
Go forth in all the earth,
embrace the path he trod,
with Christ beside
as friend and guide,
to bring good news of God.

USA © 1988 in SONGS OF DELIVERANCE by Hope Publishing Company, Carol Stream, IL 60188
World outside USA © 1985 by Timothy Dudley-Smith

HEAR HOW THE BELLS OF CHRISTMAS PLAY

Hear how the bells of Christmas play!
Well may they ring for joy and say,
　O praise him! Alleluia!
God has fulfilled his promised word,
born is our Saviour and our Lord,
　O praise him! Alleluia!

Let all the waiting earth rejoice,
lift every heart and every voice,
　O praise him! Alleluia!
Sing now the song to angels given,
Glory to God in highest heaven!
　O praise him! Alleluia!

As through the silence of the skies
shepherds in wonder heard arise,
　O praise him! Alleluia!
So may we hear again with them
songs in the night at Bethlehem,
　O praise him! Alleluia!

All nature sang at Jesus' birth
Hail the Creator come to earth!
　O praise him! Alleluia!
Sun, moon and shining stars above,
tell out the story of his love,
　O praise him! Alleluia!

Hear how the bells of Christmas play!
Well may they ring for joy and say,
　O praise him! Alleluia!
Come now to worship and adore,
Christ is our peace for evermore,
　O praise him! Alleluia!

LET EVERY CHILD OF EARTH

based on Daniel 12. 2, 3

Let every child of earth that sleeping lies
awake to hear what justice shall proclaim:
some to eternal life and light shall rise,
some to eternal shame.

Then shall they shine, for evermore the same,
the teachers of the faith, the true, the wise;
bright as the sunlit firmament aflame,
and as the starry skies.

NOT FOR TONGUES OF HEAVEN'S ANGELS

based on 1 Corinthians 13

Not for tongues of heaven's angels,
not for wisdom to discern,
not for faith that masters mountains,
for this better gift we yearn:
    may love be ours, O Lord.

Love is humble, love is gentle,
love is tender, true and kind;
love is gracious, ever patient,
generous of heart and mind:
    may love be ours, O Lord.

Never jealous, never selfish,
love will not rejoice in wrong;
never boastful nor resentful,
love believes and suffers long:
    may love be ours, O Lord.

In the day this world is fading
faith and hope will play their part;
but when Christ is seen in glory
love shall reign in every heart:
    may love be ours, O Lord.

USA © 1985 by Hope Publishing Company, Carol Stream, IL 60188
World outside USA © 1984 by Timothy Dudley-Smith

O COME TO ME, THE MASTER SAID

O come to me, the master said,
my Father knows your need;
and I shall be, the Master said,
your bread of life indeed.
 By faith in him we live and grow
 and share the broken bread
 and all his love and goodness know
 for so the Master said.

Abide in me, the Master said,
the true and living vine;
my life shall be, the Master said,
poured out for you as wine.
 His body to the cross he gave,
 his blood he freely shed,
 who came in love to seek and save,
 for so the Master said.

Believe in me, the Master said,
for I have called you friends,
and yours shall be, the Master said,
the life that never ends.
 And so, with sin and sorrow past,
 when death itself is dead,
 the Lord shall raise us up at last,
 for so the Master said.

USA © 1988 in SONGS OF DELIVERANCE by Hope Publishing Company, Carol Stream, IL 60188
World outside USA © 1987 by Timothy Dudley-Smith

OUR GOD AND FATHER BLESS

based on the Benedictus,
St. Luke 1. 68-79

Our God and Father bless,
for by his sworn decree
he sends to us in power divine
the promised Lord of David's line,
fulfilling all his love's design
to save and set us free.

His ancient purpose stands,
unchanged for evermore,
that we and all who find a place
within his covenant of grace
may freely come before his face
to worship and adore.

Let truth prepare his path,
let righteousness increase!
that from the shade of nature's night
to dawn of heaven's glory bright
the ransomed children of the light
may walk the way of peace.

OUR GOD ETERNAL, REIGNING

based on Psalm 90

Our God eternal, reigning,
creation's life sustaining,
    our refuge and our home;
enthroned, in light surrounded,
when earth was yet unfounded,
    the living God, to him we come.

We fade, a dream that passes,
like withered meadow grasses
    when summer's sun has shone.
Before that face all-seeing
of God who gave us being
    we pass away and we are gone.

O God of mercy, hear us,
in steadfast love draw near us,
    from age to age the same;
that we, by grace defended,
when earthly days are ended
    may live to praise a Saviour's Name.

PRAISE THE LORD AND BLESS HIS NAME

based on Psalm 103

Praise the Lord and bless his Name,
life and peace in him are found.
All his benefits proclaim,
grace with love and mercy crowned:
 sins forgiven, strength restored!
 Sing, my soul, and praise the Lord!

High as heaven's furthest star,
vaster than the shores of space,
so he bears our sins afar,
so he brings to us his grace.
 He who hears his children's prayer
 ever keeps us in his care.

Swifter than the winds that pass,
fading as the summer flowers,
what though all our days are grass?
faith and hope shall still be ours.
 God's unchanging love is sure
 and endures for evermore.

Praise the Lord of earth and heaven,
angel hosts about his throne,
sinners by his grace forgiven,
saints who his dominion own:
 God of all, by all adored!
 Sing, my soul, and praise the Lord!

SOFT THE EVENING SHADOWS FALL

a carol for Christmas *pilgrims*

Soft the evening shadows fall,
  still journey on;
darkness soon be over all,
  still journey on.
Weary now, and travel-worn,
night must come before the morn:
where will Mary's Son be born?
  still journey on.

Shepherds, hasten from the fold;
  this God has done.
Here in human form behold
  this God has done.
Christ the Lord of David's line,
born a Saviour and a sign,
King immortal, Child divine,
  this God has done.

Kings who from the east afar
  still journey on,
seeking Christ beneath a star,
  still journey on.
For his worship incense bring,
gold to crown an infant King,
myrrh to mark his suffering,
  still journey on.

Lord of all, enthroned above,
  God sent his Son.
Gift of everlasting love,
  God sent his Son.
He himself a ransom gave,
bowed himself to cross and grave,
came himself to seek and save,
  God sent his Son.

So the Christmas story tell;
  still journey on.
At the last shall all be well;
  still journey on.
Love be ours, and joy and praise,
one with Christ to walk his ways,
in his service all our days
  still journey on.

USA © 1987 by Hope Publishing Company, Carol Stream, IL 60188
World outside USA © 1986 by Timothy Dudley-Smith

SPIRIT OF FAITH, BY FAITH BE MINE

Spirit of faith, by faith be mine;
Spirit of truth, in wisdom shine;
Spirit of holiness divine,
    Spirit of Jesus, come!

Come to our hearts and there remain;
Spirit of life, our life sustain;
Spirit of grace and glory, reign!
    Spirit of Jesus, come!

THE EVERLASTING LORD IS KING

based on Psalm 97

The everlasting Lord is king,
  let ocean find a voice,
her furthest shores his triumph sing
and all the earth rejoice.

He comes in clouds with fire and flame
  to make his judgments known;
the mountains tremble at his Name
and melt before his throne.

The sun and moon and starry sky
  his glories blaze abroad,
the one eternal God most high,
  the true and living Lord.

Defended by his hand divine
  his saints secure remain;
for them the light of life shall shine,
  the King of love shall reign.

THE FAITHFUL ARE KEPT AS THE MOUNTAINS

based on Psalm 125, a Song of Ascents

The faithful are kept as the mountains
    that never shall move,
secure as the hills is the strength
    of the Lord and his love;
with joy they ascend, and encircled
    by mountains they come,
singing praises to God
    who is ever surrounding their home.

O Lord, our defender,
    be near in the enemy's hour,
protecting your people
    from evil's dominion and power:
as firm as the hills
    be our faith in the God we adore,
who are kept in his peace
    and surrounded by love evermore.

THE GOD OF GRACE IS OURS

based on 1 Chronicles 29. 10 - 14

The God of grace is ours,
  eternally the same,
to him be glories, honours, powers,
and blessings on his Name.

All worlds are in his hands,
all heavens his domains,
for evermore his kingdom stands
and over all he reigns.

Our good and gracious King,
from him all bounty flows;
no other gift is ours to bring
but what his love bestows.

From him our powers derive,
upon his strength we call,
beneath his hand we live and thrive,
most glorious Lord of all.

The God of grace is ours,
his holy Name we praise;
to him be glories, honours, powers,
through everlasting days.

USA © 1988 in SONGS OF DELIVERANCE by Hope Publishing Company, Carol Stream, IL 60188
World outside USA © 1985 by Timothy Dudley-Smith

THE KING OF GLORY COMES TO EARTH

The King of glory comes to earth
from God the Father given,
the heralds of his royal birth
the angel host of heaven;
    his kingly robe the swathing bands,
    his homage Mary's gaze,
    beyond the stars his kingdom stands
    to everlasting days.

The King of glory comes unknown,
the infant Lord of all;
a mother's lap his only throne,
his state a cattle stall.
    Before their naked new-born King
    the ox and ass are dumb,
    while countless choirs of angels sing
    to see his kingdom come.

The King of glory comes to die
in poverty and scorn,
upon a donkey riding by
to claim a crown of thorn.
    Creation's Lord of time and space
    is come to meet his hour,
    his triumph-song the word of grace,
    and love his only power.

The King of glory comes in peace,
and hope is ours again,
as life and love and joy increase
and faith and freedom reign.
    The Child of all our Christmas songs,
    his cross and passion past,
    will right the sum of human wrongs,
    and bring us home at last.

THE LORD IS HERE!

The Lord is here!
His promised word
is evermore the same,
 himself to be
 where two or three
are gathered in his Name.

The Lord is here!
Where Christ is come
his Spirit too is there,
 with all who raise
 the song of praise
or breathe the voice of prayer.

The Lord is here!
He comes in peace
with blessings from above,
 by pledge and sign
 of bread and wine
to fold us in his love.

The Lord is here!
To every soul
this gift of grace be given,
 to walk the way
 of Christ today,
and share the life of heaven.

USA © 1988 in SONGS OF DELIVERANCE by Hope Publishing Company, Carol Stream, IL 60188
World outside USA © 1985 by Timothy Dudley-Smith

THIS CHERISHED CHILD OF GOD'S CREATION

for the dedication of a child

This cherished child of God's creation,
 heir to a world of joy and pain,
freely in thankful dedication,
 Father, we bring to you again.

Lord, as of old the children found you,
 when to your side with joy they pressed,
so may our children gather round you
 and in your loving arms be blessed.

Spirit of holiness, descending,
 grant them to grow, as years increase,
closer to Christ and his befriending,
 filled with your love and joy and peace.

God ever One, whose care unsleeping
 watches about your children's way,
take now this child within your keeping,
 whom here we dedicate today.

WHERE DO CHRISTMAS SONGS BEGIN?

Where do Christmas songs begin?
By the stable of an inn
where the song of hosts on high
mingled with a baby's cry.
There, for joy and wonder, smiled
man and maid and holy Child.
    Christmas songs begin with them:
    sing the songs of Bethlehem!

Who is this, whose human birth
here proclaims him Child of earth?
He it is who formed the skies,
saw the new-made stars arise:
Life immortal, Light divine,
blinking in the candle-shine;
    born our darkness to dispel,
    God with us, Emmanuel!

Only love can answer why
he should come to grieve and die,
share on earth our pain and loss,
bear for us the bitter cross.
Love is come to seek and save,
Life to master death and grave,
    so in Christ is all restored,
    risen and redeeming Lord!

Praise we then, in Christmas songs
him to whom all praise belongs.
Hear the angel host reply
'Glory be to God on high,
joy and peace to mortals given,
peace on earth and peace with heaven!'
    Join we now, as one with them:
    sing the songs of Bethlehem!

WITHIN THE LOVE OF GOD I HIDE

based on Psalm 16

Within the love of God I hide,
on him my soul repose,
a tower of refuge fortified
and safe from all my foes,
a haven from the stormiest tide
and every wind that blows.

In him my true contentment lies
with those who speak his praise,
who set his face before their eyes,
his will about their ways;
the Lord my portion and my prize,
his peace on all my days.

His everlasting Name I bless,
in him my hope is stayed,
where death itself cannot distress
nor leave my soul afraid,
for in his perfect righteousness
my spirit stands arrayed.

Within my Father's purpose planned
my path of life is plain,
until before his throne I stand
and evermore remain,
where pleasures wait at his right hand,
and in his presence reign.

USA © 1988 in SONGS OF DELIVERANCE by Hope Publishing Company, Carol Stream, IL 60188
World outside USA © 1984 by Timothy Dudley-Smith

NOTES
ON THE HYMNS

Notes on the hymns

The title used for each hymn is taken from the opening line, either in full or in part. Hymn texts are in alphabetical order both when printed in full (pages 4 to 39) and in these Notes.

A city radiant as a bride   86 86 D (CMD)

Based on	Revelation 21,22
Theme	Citizens of heaven; the new Jerusalem
Written	at Ruan Minor, Cornwall, August 1986
Suggested tune	LADYWELL by William Shrubsole *or*
	FOREST GREEN Trad. English melody;
	arr. Ralph Vaughan Williams
Published in	*News of Hymnody*, January 1987 (words only)

In the *Alternative Service Book 1980* of the Church of England, 'Citizens of heaven' is the set theme for the last Sunday after Pentecost. The phrase 'fields of asphodel' (verse 2, line 4) – which was the starting point of the whole text – is a reference to Isaiah 35.2 in the New English Bible. Asphodel is traditionally the immortal flower of the Elysian fields.

Above the voices of the world around me   11 10 11 10 D

Theme	Response to the Gospel; mission and evangelism
Written	at Ruan Minor, August 1985
Suggested tune	RACHEL by Phil Burt *or*
	EXALTATION by C.H. Forest *or*
	VICAR by V. Earle Copes
Published in	*Mission Praise 2*, 1987 to RACHEL

While there are echoes in this text of many parts of Scripture, Mark 1 is dominant. See the reference in verse 1 of the text to the calling of Christ, in verse 2 to repentance in response to that call, and in verse 3 both to faith and to what Christ shall 'make me', as in Mark 1.17.

Almighty Lord Most High draw near   88 88 88

Based on	The Prayer of Manasseh
Theme	Penitence
Written	at Bramerton, January 1987
Suggested tune	MELITA by J.B. Dykes *or*
	ST. CATHERINE by Henri F. Hemy

This metrical version of part of the Prayer of Manasseh was written at the suggestion of the compilers of the American Methodist Hymnal now in preparation. The Prayer of Manasseh, one of the books of the Apocrypha, is taken to be the penitential prayer of King Manasseh of Judah described in 2 Kings. 21. 1 - 18.

An upper room with evening lamps ashine　　　　　10 10 10 10

Theme　　　　　　Holy Communion
Written　　　　　　at Ruan Minor, August 1987
Suggested tune　　FARLEY CASTLE by Henry Lawes *or*
　　　　　　　　　EVENTIDE by William H. Monk

The final verse begins with a conscious echo of the closing prayer of the Service of Holy Communion in the *Alternative Service Book 1980* of the Church of England.

Approach with awe this holiest place　　　　　　　86 86 88

Theme　　　　　　The cross of Christ; passiontide
Written　　　　　　at Ruan Minor, August 1984
Suggested tune　　PALMYRA by Joseph Summers *or*
　　　　　　　　　PEMBROKE by James Foster

The 'empty cross, empty grave', of verse 5, line 5 I owe to J.A. Motyer's book *The Message of Philippians* (IVP 1984) quoting some words of Bishop Handley Moule who wrote to a nephew in 1919:

> 'I have often prayed that daily, and to the end, I may live as in a tent pitched between the Cross and the Grave of our Lord – the *empty* Cross, symbol and seal of His finished work of sacrifice and redemption, the *empty* grave, likewise the evidence and pledge of His eternal victory for us over the last enemy, death, and of our life hid with Him in God.'

Be present, Spirit of the Lord　　　　　　　　　　86 88 6

Theme　　　　　　The Holy Spirit; Pentecost
Written　　　　　　at Bramerton, April 1984; and revised at Ruan
　　　　　　　　　Minor, August 1984
Suggested tune　　REPTON by C.H. Perry *or*
　　　　　　　　　TEILO SANT by J.P.B. Dobbs *or*
　　　　　　　　　ARNOLD by Herbert Murrill

Verse 2 echoes Isaiah 11. 1,2. 'An understanding heart' is from Solomon's prayer in 1 Kings 3.9, among other Old Testament instances.

Behold a broken world, we pray   86 86 (CM)

Based on   Micah 4. 1 - 4
Theme   The peace of the world
Written   above Poldhu Cove and at Ruan Minor, August
                1984
Suggested tune ST. MARY from Edmund Prys' *Psalter or*
                ST. FLAVIAN from John Day's *Psalmes or*
                ST. STEPHEN by William Jones *or*
                MARTYRDOM by H. Percy Smith
                and see below
Published in   *The Hymn* (Journal of the Hymn Society of
                America), July 1985 (words only)
                Singing for Peace (USA), 1986 to music by
                Douglas E. Wagner
                Anglican Praise, 1987 to ST. MARY

This text was one of the five chosen entries in the Hymn Society of
America hymn search on the theme of 'Peace', 1984/5. Among
biblical allusions notice Psalm 46.9 (verse 3, line 3); while 'the
dreamers of the day' is a phrase from T.E. Lawrence (verse 4, line
4.)

Beloved in Christ before our life began   10 10 10 10

Based on   Jeremiah 29.11
Theme   The love of God; the Christian hope
Written   at Ruan Minor, August 1985
Suggested tune See below

This short composition, together with a companion piece 'Let every
child of earth that sleeping lies', is an attempt to offer a metrical
version of a familiar scripture, as the basis of an anthem. As such, it
awaits a composer. Note the totality of God's individual provi-
dence from the phrase 'before our life began' in the first line, to 'life
for evermore' in the last.

Bless the Lord, creation sings   77 77

Based on   The Benedicite (see below)
Theme   Praise: creation
Written   begun in Holy Week 1986 at Bramerton; and
                finished at Oakworth, Yorkshire in April.
Suggested tune HARTS by Benjamin Milgrove *or*
                ST. EDMUND by Charles Steggall *or*
                MONKLAND by John Antes
Published in   *Church Family Worship*, 1986 (words only)
                Hymns for Today's Church (enlarged 2nd
                edition), 1987 to (1) HUMILITY by John Goss

(2) UNIVERSITY COLLEGE by H.J. Gauntlett.

The Benedicite, one of the canticles at Morning Prayer in the *Book of Common Prayer*, is based on part of the 'Song of the Three Holy Children' which is added in the Septuagint to the Hebrew of Daniel. A version of it appears as 'A Song of Creation' in the Order for Morning Prayer in the *Alternative Service Book 1980* of the Church of England, with a rubric suggesting substantial abbreviation for daily liturgical use. This metrical version, which was commissioned by the editors of *Hymns for Today's Church* for their second edition, can be similarly abbreviated by using only verses 1, 7 and 8. The Benedicite has been used in Christian worship from the earliest times, and by 406 was described as 'sung by Christians throughout the world'.

To a 77 77 D tune, such as ST. EDMUND, this text may be sung as four eight-line stanzas.

Christ is risen as he said   77 77

Theme   Eastertide
Written   at Ruan Minor, August 1987
Suggested tune INNOCENTS from *The Parish Choir*, 1850

In August, 1982 I wrote a Christmas antiphon, 'See, to us a child is born'; and this is intended as a companion piece. It is suggested that alternate lines might be sung by choir or soloist, with the following line by the congregation; to enhance the effect, these pairs of lines begin with the same word. Besides the ressurrection accounts in the gospels, biblical allusions include Colossians 1.18, Revelation 17.14, Philippians 2. 10,11, Romans 8.2, 2 Corinthians 2.14, Luke 19.10.

Come and see where Jesus lay   77 77 D

Based on   Matthew 28. 6,7
Theme   Eastertide; mission and evangelism
Written   at Poldhu and Ruan Minor, August 1986
Suggested tune ST. EDMUND by Charles Steggall *or*
                EVERLASTING LOVE by James Mountain

The structure, as can be seen, is designed to emphasize the two imperatives of verses 6 & 7 in Matthew 28. 'Telling' is to be based on first-hand evidence of 'seeing'.

Eye has not seen, nor ear has heard   86 86 (CM)

Theme   The love and wisdom of God
Written   at Ruan Minor, August 1985
Suggested tune CAITHNESS from the *Scottish Psalter*, 1635 *or*

ST. AGNES by John B. Dykes

While one could not describe this text as 'based on' 1 Corinthians 2. 9,10, its origin lies there. In the final verse there are echoes of 1 Corinthians 3.21, 1 Thessalonians 4.17, and Ephesians 3.18,19. Isaac Watts, I have since noted, wrote a hymn in his *Hymns and Spiritual Songs* 1707, beginning 'Nor Eye has seen, nor Ear has heard'.

For peace with God above   66 66

Based on   Philippians 4
Theme   Peace and blessing; love for God
Written   at Ruan Minor, August 1984
Suggested tune   IBSTONE by Maria Tiddeman *or*
                  CORROUR BOTHY by Caryl Micklem

The three verses speak of the peace of God, of peace with God, and of the God of peace. The first and third are in Philippians 4. 7 & 9, and the middle one in, for example, Romans 5.1.

From all the wind's wide quarters   76 76 D

Based on   Isaiah 55
Theme   The feast of life; redemption and deliverance
Written   at Ruan Minor and Poldhu Cove, August 1984
Suggested tune   CRÜGER by Johannes Crüger *or*
                  AURELIA by S.S. Wesley

The phrase 'feast of life' is borrowed from the title of a book by Canon John Poulton;[1.] but used here in the sense of the 'gospel feast'.

In John Wesley's *A Collection of Hymns for the Use of the People called Methodists* of 1780, No. 2 is 'Come, sinners, to the gospel feast' and No. 4 is based on Isaiah 55.

[1.] *The Feast of Life – A Theological Reflection on the Theme: Jesus Christ, the Life of the World*, by John Poulton (World Council of Churches, Geneva, 1982)

From the Father's throne on high   77 77

Based on   Mark 13. 24-27
Theme   Advent; the return of Christ in glory
Written   at Bramerton, January 1986
Suggested tune   SONG 13 by Orlando Gibbons *or*
                  ORIENTIS PARTIBUS by Pierre de Corbeil *or*
                  MONKLAND by John Antes
Published in   *Carol Praise*, 1987 to MONKLAND

Note the reference in verse 1 to the first and second advents of Christ; and in verse 5 to Christ's inauguration both of the created world, and of the new age.

From the night of ages waking   87 87 87

Theme   Christ our Light
Written   at Bramerton, January 1987
Suggested tune REGENT SQUARE by Henry Smart

In August 1987 the International Fellowship of Evangelical Students held their General Committee in Colombia. For this international gathering I was asked to write a hymn on the theme of the conference. 'Jesus Christ, the Light of the world'. A number of bible passages from which the hymn is drawn can be readily identified: e.g. Isaiah 9 & 60; Psalm 27; and the Gospel of John. 'Shined' in verse 1, is a deliberate archaism to echo the King James (AV) version of 2 Corinthians 4.6.

Give thanks to God on high   66 86 66

Theme   Thanksgiving, anniversary, dedication, saints and
                forerunners.
Written   at Ruan Minor, August 1984
Suggested tune VINEYARD HAVEN by Richard Dirkson *or*
                CHRISTO ET REGNO by Daniel Horn
Recorded on   Cassette album 8504-0104, Wheaton College
                recording, 1985, to CHRISTO ET REGNO

This text was requested by Wheaton College, Illinois, for their 125th anniversary, and was first sung at the Anniversary Convocation on January 9th 1985 in the Edman Memorial Chapel. The tune CHRISTO ET REGNO was composed for this text by Daniel Horn, a Faculty member of the Wheaton College Conservatory of Music. 'For Christ and his kingdom' is the College motto.

God and Father, ever giving   87 87 77

Theme   The Holy Trinity; praise and worship
Written   at Ruan Minor, August 1987
Suggested tune ALL SAINTS (German traditional)

The trinitarian address of the first three verses is echoed in the threefold reference to 'the life we share'; so that it is shared in our creation by the Father (Genesis 2.7); and in union with Christ the Son (2 Corinthians 5.17); and in the indwelling of the Spirit (Romans 8.11).

Good news of God above   66 86 D (SMD)

Theme   Mission and evangelism
Written   at Ruan Minor, August 1985
Suggested tune   ICH HALTE TREULICH STILL attributed to
                 J.S. Bach *or*
                 DIADEMATA by George J. Elvey

Note in verse 4 line 4, 'make known, declare, proclaim', a reference
to each of the preceding verses with the 'make known' from verse 1
line 9, 'declare' from verse 3 line 6, and 'proclaim' from verse 2 line
1.

Hear how the bells of Christmas play   88 44 88 and Alleluias

Theme   Christmas
Written   at Ruan Minor, August 1985
Suggested tune   EASTER SONG (or LASST UNS ERFREUEN),
                 Cologne 1623
Published in   *Carol Praise*, 1987 to EASTER SONG

It had been in my mind for a little time that EASTER SONG, with
its exuberance and rejoicing would make a good tune for a Christmas hymn. Although at certain times and places the liturgical
alleluia ('Praise the Lord') has been especially associated with
Easter, it also seems highly appropriate for the nativity. I have
attempted, where possible, to make the third and sixth lines more
than an interjection, so that they become part of the construction of
the verse. It is what the bells proclaim (verse 1), what our voices
sing (verse 2), what the angels heard (verse 3) and what nature
expresses (verse 4).

Let every child of earth that sleeping lies   10 10 10 6

Based on   Daniel 12. 2,3
Theme   Judgment; church and ministry
Written   at Ruan Minor, August 1985
Suggested tune   MUNDAYS by Martin Shaw

The second in the pair of texts described in the note to 'Beloved in
Christ before our world began' on page 11. Note how verse 2
employs the same rhymes as verse 1, but in reverse order.

Not for tongues of heaven's angels   87 87 6

Based on   1 Corinthians 13
Theme   Love
Written   at Ruan Minor, August 1984
Suggested tune   BRIDEGROOM by Peter Cutts
Published in   *New Songs of Praise 1*, 1985 to BRIDEGROOM

Worship III (USA), 1986 to BRIDEGROOM

Written as a text on love for *New Songs of Praise*; and to the tune BRIDEGROOM at the request of Robert Batastini, then preparing *Worship III*.

O come to me, the Master said   86 86 D (CMD)

Theme	Christian experience and discipleship; Holy Communion.
Written	at Ruan Minor, August 1987
Suggested tune	KINGSFOLD (Traditional) *or* ALL SAINTS NEW by Henry S. Cutler

New Testament references include Matthew 11.28 ('Come to me . . .'); John 15.4 ('Abide in me . . .'); and John 14.1 ('Believe also in me . . .'). The 'bread of life' of verse 1 and the 'raising up' of verse 3 are both from John 6.

Our God and Father bless   66 888 6

Based on	The Benedictus, Luke 1. 68 - 79
Theme	Redemption
Written	at Bramerton and Ruan Minor, August 1986
Suggested tune	see below.

This is my second attempt at a metrical Benedictus, the first being among the 'Discontinued texts' of Appendix 6 to *Lift Every Heart*. No tune seems to be known to this metre.

Our God eternal, reigning   776 778

Based on	Psalm 90
Theme	God the Father; the living God
Written	at Ruan Minor, August 1987
Suggested tune	INNSBRUCK by Heinrich Isaak

It is a daunting task to write a modern metrical version of Psalm 90, the original of Isaac Watts' 'Our God, our help in ages past'. This attempt was for a new book of metrical psalms in preparation; and the tune INNSBRUCK was one I had been wanting to write to. It can be seen that (as with Isaac Watts) it is scarcely possible to include all of the Psalm. Watts' intention to see 'David converted into a Christian' can be noticed in the final line of the text.

Praise the Lord and bless his Name   77 77 77

Based on	Psalm 103
Theme	Praise and worship; trust in God
Written	at Ruan Minor, August 1986
Suggested tune	WELLS by D.S. Bortnianski *or*

DIX by Conrad Kocher

Like the preceding text, this stands in the shadow of a great and familiar hymn, in this case Henry Lyte's version 'Praise, my soul, the King of heaven'. Verse 3 of my text is a reminder of a verse of Lyte's omitted in most modern hymnals, beginning 'Frail as summer's flower we flourish'.

Soft the evening shadows fall   74 74 7774

Theme	Christmas; 'a carol for Christmas pilgrims'
Written	at Ruan Minor, August 1986
Suggested tune	THE MARCH OF THE CHRISTMAS PILGRIMS by Michael Paget *or* SOUTHGATE by T.B. Southgate
Published in	*Carol Praise*, 1987 to THE MARCH OF THE CHRISTMAS PILGRIMS

First printed on our family Christmas card for 1986, this text proved popular as a challenge to composers, and I have on file a number of tunes in MS. The subtitle, 'A carol for Christmas pilgrims' serves to draw the mind on from the events of Christmas to the demands of everyday discipleship at the start of a new year.

Spirit of faith, by faith be mine   888 6

Theme	The Holy Spirit
Written	at Ruan Minor, August 1985
Suggested tune	SAFFRON WALDEN by A.H. Brown *or* FLEMMING by Friedrich F. Flemming

The RSV biblical references for these titles are:

Spirit of faith - 2 Corinthians 4.13
Spirit of truth - John 14.17
Spirit of holiness - Romans 1.4
Spirit of Jesus - Philippians 1.19
Spirit of life - Romans 8.2
Spirit of grace - Hebrews 10.29
Spirit of glory - 1 Peter 4.14

The everlasting Lord is king   86 86 (CM)

Based on	Psalm 97
Theme	God the Father; the living God
Written	at Ruan Minor, August 1987
Suggested tune	KILMARNOCK by Neil Dougall *or* CAMPMEETING Trad. American melody. Arr. Robert McCutchan

Isaac Watts' version of this Psalm, in accordance with his principles

of versification, contains the line:
'In Britain is Jehovah known'.

The faithful are kept as the mountains   14 14 14 15

Based on   Psalm 125
Theme   God our strength
Written   at Ruan Minor, August 1987
Suggested tune   SHEEN by Gustav Holst

Psalm 125, 'a Song of Ascents', was used by pilgrims on their way
to the temple at Jerusalem. John Stott in *The Canticles & Selected
Psalms* (Hodder & Stoughton, 1966) sums up the two mountain
metaphors of this psalm which I have tried to bring out in these two
verses: 'God's people are like a mountain surrounded by mountains, both immovable and impregnable.'

The God of grace is ours   66 86 (SM)

Based on   1 Chronicles 29. 10 - 14
Theme   Praise & worship; thanksgiving; stewardship
Written   at Ruan Minor, August 1985
Suggested tune   VENICE by William Amps *or*
                 CARLISLE by Charles Lockhart *or*
                 ST. BRIDE by Samuel Howard *or*
                 FESTAL SONG by William H. Walter

David's prayer at the inauguration of Solomon's temple has pro-
vided words of thanksgiving which God's people have used ever
since – see for example the ascription set for the offering in the
Holy Communion Service of the *Alternative Service Book 1980* of
the Church of England (page 129).

The King of glory comes to earth   86 86 D (CMD)

Theme   Christmas
Written   at Ruan Minor, August 1987
Suggested tune   KINGSFOLD (traditional)

Written for our family Christmas card, 1987.

The Lord is here!   446 446 *or*
                                                            86 86 (CM)

Theme   Holy Communion; praise & worship
Written   at Ruan Minor, August 1985
Suggested tune   STRACATHRO by Charles Hutcheson *or*
                 DUNDEE from Ravenscroft's Psalms

The words 'The Lord is here!' mark the beginning of the Eucharistic Prayer in the Holy Communion Service, Rite A, of the *Alternative Service Book 1980* of the Church of England.

This cherished child of God's creation   98 98

Theme   for the dedication of a child
Written   at Ruan Minor, August 1986
Suggested tune   SPIRITUS VITAE by Mary Hammond *or*
                   LES COMMENDEMENS from Strasbourg, 1545
                   or
                   EUCHARISTIC HYMN by John S.B. Hodges
Published in   *New Songs of Praise 3*, to SPIRITUS VITAE

Written in response to the Oxford University Press search for hymns on this theme for inclusion in *New Songs of Praise 3*, the hymn is intended for use in a Service of Dedication, either in churches which do not practice infant baptism, or where dedication is preferred, as in the 'Service of Thanksgiving for the Birth of a Child' in the *Alternative Service Book 1980* of the Church of England. The problem of gender ('him/her') has been avoided by casting verses 2, 3, and 4a into the plural. Note the Trinitarian form, summed up in the words 'God ever One'. I owe the adjective 'cherished' to Derek Kidner.

Where do Christmas songs begin?   77 77 D

Theme   Christmas
Written   at Poldhu Cove and Ruan Minor, August 1984
Suggested tune   MAIDSTONE by W.B. Gilbert *or*
                   ST. EDMUND by Charles Steggall *or*
                   ABERYSTWYTH by Joseph Parry
Published in   *Carol Praise*, 1987 to MOUNTAIN HEIGHTS
                   (composer unknown)

A Christmas carol based on the questions Where? Who? Why?

Within the love of God I hide   86 86 86

Based on   Psalm 16
Theme   Testimony; confidence; hope
Written   at Ruan Minor, August 1984
Suggested tune   BRUNSWICK adapted from G.F. Handel *or*
                   SHELTERED DALE (German traditional)

Psalm 16 has been called 'a believer's testimony regarding both his present faith and his future hope'. Charles Wesley's 'Forth in thy name' drew on this psalm.

INDEXES

- HYMNALS
- BIBLICAL REFERENCES
- METRE
- SUGGESTED TUNES
- SUBJECTS
- FIRST LINES

Index of hymnals

containing texts appearing in this collection

New Songs of Praise 1   Oxford University Press, Oxford 1985
Not for tongues of heaven's angels

Worship III   GIA Publications Inc., Chicago USA 1986
Not for tongues of heaven's angels

Singing for Peace   Hope Publishing Co., Carol Stream, Illinois USA 1986
Behold a broken world, we pray

Church Family Worship   Hodder & Stoughton, London 1986
Bless the Lord, creation sings

New Songs of Praise 3   Oxford University Press, Oxford 1987
This cherished child of God's creation

Mission Praise 2   Marshall Morgan and Scott, Basingstoke, Hants 1987
Above the voices of the world around me

Anglican Praise   Oxford University Press, Oxford 1987
Behold a broken world, we pray

Carol Praise   Marshall Morgan and Scott, Basingstoke, Hants 1987
From the Father's throne on high
Hear how the bells of Christmas play
Soft the evening shadows fall
Where do Christmas songs begin?

Hymns for Today's Church   (enlarged 2nd edition) Hodder & Stoughton, London 1987
Bless the Lord, creation sings

Periodicals

The Hymn   Journal of the Hymn Society of America, July 1985
Behold a broken world, we pray

News of Hymnody   January 1987
A city radiant as a bride

Music in Worship   Autumn 1987 ('Carol Praise' Supplement)
Soft the evening shadows fall

Index of Biblical references

Please see the Foreword for further details.

1 Chronicles	29. 10-14	The God of grace is ours
Psalm	16	Within the love of God I hide
Psalm	90	Our God eternal, reigning
Psalm	97	The everlasting Lord is king
Psalm	103	Praise the Lord and bless his Name
Psalm	125	The faithful are kept as the mountains
Isaiah	55	From all the wind's wide quarters
Jeremiah	29. 11	Beloved in Christ before our world began
Daniel	12. 2,3	Let every child of earth that sleeping lies
Micah	4	Behold a broken world, we pray
Matthew	11. 28	O come to me, the Master said
Matthew	28. 6,7	Come and see where Jesus lay
Mark	13. 24-27	From the Father's throne on high
Luke	1. 68-79	Our God and Father bless
John	6 & 15	O come to me, the Master said
1 Corinthians	2. 9	Eye has not seen, nor ear has heard
1 Corinthians	13	Not for tongues of heaven's angels
Philippians	4	For peace with God above
Revelation	21, 22	A city radiant as a bride

From the Apocrypha

The Song of the Three Holy Children, 35-66	Bless the Lord, creation sings
The Prayer of Manasseh	Almighty Lord Most High draw near

Canticles

A Song of Creation	the name used in the Church of England *Alternative Service Book 1980* for the Benedicite.
Benedicite	see the Song of the Three Holy Children under *Apocrypha* above
Benedictus	see Luke 1. 68 - 79 above

Metrical index

This follows the classification used in *Lift Every Heart*.
Metres not represented there are marked *.

*446 446
The Lord is here!

66 66
For peace with God above

66 86 (Short Metre : SM)
The God of grace is ours

66 86 66
Give thanks to God on high

*66 86 D (Double Short Metre : SMD)
Good news of God above

*66 888 6
Our God and Father bless

*74 74 777 4
Soft the evening shadows fall

76 76 D
From all the wind's wide quarters

*776 778
Our God eternal, reigning

77 77
Bless the Lord, creation sings
Christ is risen as he said
From the Father's throne on high

77 77 77
Praise the Lord and bless his Name

77 77 D
Come and see where Jesus lay
Where do Christmas songs begin?

86 86 (Common Metre : CM)
Behold a broken world, we pray
Eye has not seen, nor ear has heard
The everlasting Lord is king
The Lord is here!

*86 86 86
Within the love of God I hide

86 86 D (Double Common Metre : CMD)
A city radiant as a bride
O come to me, the Master said
The King of glory comes to earth

86 86 88
Approach with awe this holiest place

86 88 6
Be present, Spirit of the Lord

*87 87 6
Not for tongues of heaven's angels

87 87 77
God and Father, ever giving

87 87 87
From the night of ages waking

*88 44 88 and Alleluias
Hear how the bells of Christmas play

*888 6
Spirit of faith, by faith be mine

88 88 88
Almighty Lord Most High draw near

*98 98
This cherished child of God's creation

10 10 10 6
Let every child of earth that sleeping lies

10 10 10 10
An upper room with evening lamps ashine
Beloved in Christ before our life began

11 10 11 10 D
Above the voices of the world around me

*14 14 14 15
The faithful are kept as the mountains

Index of suggested tunes

Tunes to which texts have been set in the published hymnals
listed on page 54 are marked *.

ABERYSTWYTH
Where do Christmas songs begin?

ALL SAINTS
God and Father, ever giving

ALL SAINTS NEW
O come to me, the Master said

ARNOLD
Be present, Spirit of the Lord

AURELIA
From all the wind's wide quarters

*BRIDEGROOM
Not for tongues of heaven's angels

BRUNSWICK
Within the love of God I hide

CAITHNESS
Eye has not seen, nor ear has heard

CAMPMEETING
The everlasting Lord is king

CARLISLE
The God of grace is ours

*CHRISTO ET REGNO
Give thanks to God on high

CORROUR BOTHY
For peace with God above

CRÜGER
From all the wind's wide quarters

DIADEMATA
Good news of God above

DIX
Praise the Lord and bless his Name

DUNDEE
The Lord is here!

*EASTER SONG
Hear how the bells of Christmas play

EUCHARISTIC HYMN
This cherished child of God's creation

EVENTIDE
An upper room with evening lamps ashine

EVERLASTING LOVE
Come and see where Jesus lay

EXALTATION
Above the voices of the world around me

FARLEY CASTLE
An upper room with evening lamps ashine

FESTAL SONG
The God of grace is ours

FLEMMING
Spirit of faith, by faith be mine

FOREST GREEN
A city radiant as a bride

HARTS
Bless the Lord, creation sings

*HUMILITY
Bless the Lord, creation sings

IBSTONE
For peace with God above

ICH HALTE TREULICH STILL
Good news of God above

INNOCENTS
Christ is risen as he said

INNSBRUCK
Our God eternal, reigning

KILMARNOCK
The everlasting Lord is king

KINGFOLD
O come to me, the Master said
The King of glory comes to earth

LADYWELL
A city radiant as a bride

*LASST UNS ERFREUEN - see EASTER SONG

LES COMMENDEMENS
This cherished child of God's creation

MAIDSTONE
Where do Christmas songs begin?

MARTYRDOM
Behold a broken world

MELITA
Almighty Lord Most High draw near

*MONKLAND
Bless the Lord, creation sings
From the Father's throne on high

*MOUNTAIN HEIGHTS
Where do Christmas songs begin?

MUNDAYS
Let every child of earth that sleeping lies

ORIENTIS PARTIBUS
From the Father's throne on high

PALMYRA
Approach with awe this holiest place

PEMBROKE
Approach with awe this holiest place

*RACHEL
Above the voices of the world around me

REGENT SQUARE
From the night of ages waking

REPTON
Be present, Spirit of the Lord

SAFFRON WALDEN
Spirit of faith, by faith be mine

ST. AGNES
Eye has not seen, nor ear has heard

ST. BRIDE
The God of grace is ours

ST. CATHERINE
Almighty Lord Most High draw near

ST. EDMUND
Bless the Lord, creation sings
Come and see where Jesus lay
Where do Christmas songs begin?

ST. FLAVIAN
Behold a broken world, we pray

*ST. MARY
Behold a broken world, we pray

ST. STEPHEN
Behold a broken world, we pray

SHEEN
The faithful are kept as the mountains

SHELTERED DALE
Within the love of God I hide

SONG 13
From the Father's throne on high

SOUTHGATE
Soft the evening shadows fall

*SPIRITUS VITAE
This cherished child of God's creation

STRACATHRO
The Lord is here!

*THE MARCH OF THE CHRISTMAS PILGRIMS
Soft the evening shadows fall

TEILO SANT
Be present, Spirit of the Lord

*UNIVERSITY COLLEGE
Bless the Lord, creation sings

VENICE
The God of grace is ours

VICAR
Above the voices of the world around me

VINEYARD HAVEN
Give thanks to God on high

WELLS
Praise the Lord and bless his Name

I maintain a file of MS music sent to me by composers who have written tunes to my texts, and will gladly send details to editors or others who may wish to consult it.

TDS

Index of subjects

This follows the classification used in *Lift Every Heart*.
New categories are marked *.

*Incarnation
See: Christmas and Epiphany

*Judgment
Let every child of earth that sleeping lies

*Light
See: Christ our Light

Living God
See: God the Father: the living God

*Love
Not for tongues of heaven's angels

Love for God
For peace with God above
God and Father, ever giving

Love of God
Beloved in Christ before our world began
Eye has not seen, nor ear has heard
Within the love of God I hide

Mission & Evangelism
Above the voices of the world around me
Come and see where Jesus lay
From all the wind's wide quarters
Good news of God above

Nature
Bless the Lord, creation sings

*New Jerusalem
A city radiant as a bride

New life in Christ
Above the voices of the world around me
From all the wind's wide quarters
Good news of God above

Passiontide
Approach with awe this holiest place
Eye has not seen, nor ear has heard

Peace
See: Confidence and peace

*Peace of the world
Behold a broken world, we pray

Penitence
Above the voices of the world around me
Almighty Lord Most High draw near

Pentecost
Be present, Spirit of the Lord
Spirit of faith, by faith be mine

Praise and Worship
Bless the Lord, creation sings
God and Father, ever giving
Praise the Lord and bless his Name
The God of grace is ours
The Lord is here!

Redemption
Approach with awe this holiest place
For peace with God above
From all the wind's wide quarters
Our God and Father bless

Renewal
See: Dedication and Renewal

*Response to the Gospel
Above the voices of the world around me

Resurrection
See: Eastertide

*Return of Christ in glory
See: Advent

*Saints
Give thanks to God on high

*Stewardship
The God of grace is ours

*Testimony
Within the love of God I hide

Thanksgiving
Give thanks to God on high
The God of grace is ours

Trinity
See: Holy Trinity

Trust in God
See: Confidence and peace

*Whitsun
See: Pentecost

Wisdom of God
Eye has not seen, nor ear has heard

Index of First Lines